COLOR
of my
SKIN

Liz Baker

Inspired 4 U Publications
www.howtoselfpublishinexcellence.com

COLOR *of my* **SKIN**

Copyright © 2019 Liz Baker

All rights reserved. No portion of this book may be reproduced, stored in a retrieval system, or transmitted in any form or by any means electronic, photocopying, recording or otherwise without prior written permission of the author upon request at PoetryofLiz@gmail.com.

ISBN-13: 978-0-9994252-6-8

DEDICATION

"Color *of my* Skin" is dedicated to the Black Men and Women who have lost their lives to racism.

*"Darkness cannot drive out darkness:
only light can do that. Hate cannot drive out hate:
only love can do that."*

- Martin Luther King Jr

Contents

Acknowledgments i
Preface iii
[Untitled] 1
Who Am I? 3
Meaning of Black and Brown 4
Victim 5
Over 400 Years 6
African American History 7
Sheets Off 9
A Black Man's Daily Prayer 11
Modern Day 13
Racially Asinine 14
Hail 15
No Nation 16
War 17
Don't Shoot Me 18
The Shadows 19
You People 21
Don't Judge Me 23
The Jury 25
Young Man 27

Mommy	28
Where I Come From	29
Disappearing Race	30
Nigger Vs. Nigga	31
Once Upon A Time	33
Black On Black	35
Wounded Children	36
Father	37
Walk In My Shoes	39
No Color	41
Letter To The Police	43
No More Flags	45
Black List	47
Conspiracy	49
Call The Police?!	51
Struggles	53
Growing Up	54
Black and Powerful	55
Men	57
Why?	59
We Shall Overcome	61
Words Have Power	62
Futuristic	63

Addicted 65

Hard Being Black 67

Guilty Plea 68

Rest In Peace 69

About The Author 75

"Men are so constituted that they derive their conviction of their own possibilities largely from the estimate formed of them by others. If nothing is expected of a people, that people will find it difficult to contradict that expectation."

- Frederick Douglass

ACKNOWLEDGMENTS

I want to thank God for where I've been and where He's placed me now. If it weren't for God, nothing that I'm doing would be possible. He placed people in my path as guardian angels, who watched over me.

God blessed me with a wonderful mother, Lezette Clark, who never neglected me for drugs. She stuck by my side through thick and thin. God personally assigned her to be my provider, protector, and teacher. Without God and my mother's guidance, I don't know where I would have ended up in life.

To my mentors: Along with the teachings of my mother, you helped me set a bar and excel. Mr. Williams, Mr. Dyson, and Ms. Hallinan, words cannot express the gratitude and appreciation I have for each of you. You encouraged me, never gave up on me, and taught me the values of the real world. God placed you three angels in my life, and you caused me to accomplish a great deal throughout my childhood, youthful days, and adulthood. My mother entrusted me with you, and you made sure I was safe and nurtured in your care.

Mr. Pretlow, I also thank you for everything you did for me. If it weren't for you, I would not have been discovered and gone to school on a scholarship. You took a huge chance on me and caused me to flourish.

God puts people in our paths, and I'm grateful you were the right kind of people who crossed mine. You each believed in me when no one else did, and you saw something that I never saw in myself. I thank all of you and love you to the moon and back!

PREFACE

"Color *of my* Skin" was written for my people, not for personal recognition or attention. I wrote this book to draw attention to the issues of being Black in America and the Black community. My people are targets, and it feels as if we've been made the number one enemy in America.

The inspiration for "Color *of my* Skin" came from what was happening to unarmed Black men and women, who have been killed by the hands of Law Enforcement Officers. It angered me that the very people we look to for protection were committing murderous crimes because of race and the color of our skin. They frequently perpetrate extreme measures against Black people, and we are "feared" because of the media's negative portrayal of us and institutionalized racism. Graphic, undeniable video footage of many violent occurrences of police encounters goes ignored, without justice for the victims or their families.

Additionally, it feels as if we're conditioned to hate each other and put one another down. But, our ancestors did not suffer and die for us to kill one another. Open your eyes people! Each of us must make choices for ourselves that no one else can make for us.

"The past is ghost, the future a dream. All we ever have is now."
- Bill Cosby

[UNTITLED]

When I look in the mirror, I see dark skin,
brown eyes, black kinky hair.

My skin, silky smooth;
spaced teeth, pretty smile.

Acne-free face, free of bumps,
no bags, clear eyes.

My hair flows naturally down my back.
I smell good, nicely groomed, well-kept.
Mind clear, thoughts good, great intellect.

Very educated, graduated,
two degrees magna cum laude.
Nice person, great heart,
ask all who know about me.

Honest living, pay taxes,
never went to prison.

Husband, children, big house, and
nice retirement is what I envision.

Family woman, love children, love nice cars,
love electronics and gadgets.

Homebody, sports lover, movie watcher,
spades player, and good at it.

Nice dresser, love to shop;
take care of the ones I love.

Take pictures, love to travel,
and love to laugh.

Brown skin, brown eyes, black hair.

I go all out and live everyday
like it's my last.

WHO AM I?

Am I a slave, picking cotton?
Am I a rapist, raping women and children?
Am I the dirty Black you call a "nigger"?
Am I a killer, killing people?
Am I an abusive person?
Am I a high school drop out?
Am I the drug dealer, selling drugs?
Am I a thief, robbing people?
Am I the ex-con, in and out of prison?
Am I the one on public assistance?
Am I the person you see on the news?
Am I a failure to society?
Am I a thug in red or blue, throwing up signs?
Am I just another statistic?
Am I destined to be killed by cops?
Who Am I?
Would it matter if I were white?

MEANING OF BLACK AND BROWN

B   is for Bonafide authenticity.

L   is for Liberated souls.

A   is for Ambitious characteristics.

C   is for Captivating personalities.

K   is for Keen manifestations.

B   is Bodacious, Bountiful, Blessed, Brilliant…

R   is Radiant, Receptive, Remarkable, Real…

O   is Outstanding, Original, Open-Minded, Opulent…

W   is Wise, Whole, Worthy, Wonderful…

N   is Nourishing, Noble, Nifty, Nice...

VICTIM

So, aren't I a victim because of the news?
When they downplay where I come from?
Or because I am a "certain kind" of people?
Because I'm hard to relate to?

Or is it because of the stereotypes of my culture?
So, they stop and frisk me,
or slam me to the floor.

When they judge me based on
what they read in a magazine?

Or when I pass, they clutch their purses?
And move when I take a seat?

Or accuse me as the perpetrator
because I fit the description?

Shoot me when I have my hands up?

Give me stares because
they think I'm corrupt?

Who is the real victim?

Aren't I a victim of these cruel stereotypes?

I am my own person, judging me isn't right!

OVER 400 YEARS

Born a slave to work for "The Man."

Torn from families, broken into pieces.

Placed in fields to pick Cotton.

Robbed of their land, home, and dignity.

Hung on trees, whipped and beaten.

Placed in the "hood and ghettos," and
behind prison walls, separated from family.

Built up, then torn down.

Gentrification all around town.

The displacement of poor communities
by rich outsiders.

Shot and killed, caught up in conspiracies.

No room for growth because people are intimidated.

Poor schools for poor people.

Bad education, deprived of learning.

Over 400 hundred years, and this keeps on going.

AFRICAN AMERICAN HISTORY

Crispus Attucks (1723-1770) was the first person killed in the Boston Massacre for American Freedom.

Elizabeth Freeman (1744-1829) was the first enslaved African American to file and win a freedom suit in Massachusetts. Slavery was found to be inconsistent with the 1780 State Constitution.

Paul Cuffee (1759-1817) won the right to vote in Massachusetts for taxpaying landowners of color.

Richard Allen (1760-1831) founded the first independent Black denomination, African Methodist Episcopal (AME) Church, in the U.S. in 1794.

James Forten (1766 -1842) was an abolitionist and wealthy businessman. Born free in PA, he became a sail-maker, who invented a device that improved the handling of sails.

Samuel E. Cornish (1795-1858) and **John B. Russwurm** (1799-1851) founded the first Black-owned and operated newspaper in America, Freedom's Journal in 1827.

Sojourner Truth (1797-1883) was born Isabella Baumfree, and was an abolitionist and women's rights advocate.

Nat Turner (1800-1831) fought for freedom and led a two-day rebellion of slaves and free Blacks. He made it clear that African Americans would get freedom one way or another. He was hanged.

Lewis Howard Latimer (1848-1928) drafted the patent drawings for Alexander Graham Bell's telephone invention. He also invented a method of making carbon filaments for the Maxim electric incandescent lamp; an supervised the installation of electric lights in NY, PA, MTL, LDN.

Nat Love (1851-1921) was a Black Cowboy. His exploits have made him one of the most famous Black heroes of the Old West.

Dr. Daniel Hale Williams (1851-1931) performed the first successful American open-heart surgery.

Granville T. Woods (1856-1910) invented a telegraph that sends messages to moving trains, the light dimmer, the electromagnetic brake telephone transmitter, and an electrified component that allows railcars to operate underground as subways. His technology was bought by General Electric, American Bell Telephone….

Madame C.J. Walker (1867-1919) developed the hot comb and created her own beauty shops. She had thousands of people that worked for her. With her success and money, she donated to the Tuskegee Institute.

History never learned in the classrooms
at public school, but learned in an HBCU.
I love my Historically Black Colleges
for teaching me my roots:
Who I am as a Black woman
and the Black man's true identity,
Not the false discovery of America
by a European thief.

SHEETS OFF

The white sheets with the eyes cut out are gone.

No more white sheets with the pointy top.

No more burned crosses and bricks
thrown through windows.

People sitting on horses are long gone.

People hanging from trees with whip marks.

When the sheets come off,
the blue uniforms come out.

Black robes banging the gavel, giving life sentences.

People in white and blue cars killing people.

The dominant power robbing people,
and paying them less wages.

No more house "niggers," or hanging them.

Just blatantly slaughter them with bombs
like the Four Little Girls.

Now 9 people shot dead in broad daylight.
Was on the news when it first happened,
but suddenly disappeared.

Just like crimes against "niggers" never reappears!

*"Cops give a damn about a negro.
Pull the trigger, kill a nigga, he's a hero.
Give the crack to the kids, who the hell cares?
One less hungry mouth on the welfare!"*

- Tupac Shakur

A BLACK MAN'S DAILY PRAYER

Lord, I thank you for making me
into a strong man.

Blessings and glory, Lord,
that I'm not a statistic, or a
product of my environment,
standing on the corner slanging, or
killing my own kind with guns banging.

I thank you, Lord, for the strength
you have given me in this tough world
that is so anti-Black!

I thank you, Lord, for sparing my life.
There are lots of people who wish me dead.

I thank you, Lord,
that I'm able to provide
for my family like a man.
This cold world just don't understand
the day in and day out struggles
of a free Black man.

Lord give me strength, and protect me
from being wrongly accused of rape,
murder, robbery, and assault, and from
being shot for loud music, or being shot
in the head by people who wear badges,
or being beaten by the police,

or being sentenced to a life sentence
for a crime I never committed!

I thank you, Lord,
for choosing my paths.
Because of you, I graduated high school,
and got a college degree.
Now I'm working for a multi-million dollar company.

I thank you, Lord,
for seeing my heart beyond my flesh.
I'm not a perfect man Lord,
but you don't judge my mistakes or failures,
because I know that I need you; and I know
not to lean on my own understanding.

Thank you, Lord,
for allowing me to provide for my family,
and for blessing me beyond measure.
My success is my treasure.
Not of this world, but my ability
to make a living in this cold world.

Thank you, Lord,
for all that you are allowing me to do.
I'd be dead or in jail if it weren't for You!

Amen.

MODERN DAY

Is this modern day slavery?

Instead of being sprayed with hoses,
We are sprayed with bullets.

Instead of whips and ropes,
We are tased and choked.

We are ripped and dragged away
from our families.

Increasing deaths from police brutality.

Cops stopping anyone who fits the description.

Shoot first ask later, different time, same fight.

A world of liberty, yet no peace.

Freedom of speech, but words unheard.

Associates, Bachelors, Masters, Doctorate…
But seen differently, not even moderate.

Clothes I wear, how I look, dress, talk.
Forget I own businesses or am an actor.
Seen as a thief and followed in stores.

Need I say more?

RACIALLY ASININE

"Six against one," Jena 6.

One kills nine, genocide.

"Six against one," racist.

One kills nine, the act of terrorist.

"Six against one," criminal – convict – assassin.

One kills nine, now labeled victim.

"Six against one," racial injustice.

One kills nine, no justice.

"Six against one," gangsters – thugs.

One kills nine, mentally unstable.

Different folks, different labels.

HAIL

I reach forward and stick my hand out,
Looking forward, sideways, front and back.
I see other people doing the same.

Thirty minutes pass, forty minutes pass.
For them they stop, for them they came.
As I stick my hand out, lights go off,
And all of a sudden, there's a shift change.

Black, yellow, green midsize cars and vans.
All pass me by. With my hand out, I stand.
None of them stop for me.

I have money. I work. I pay taxes.
I pay my bills on time. I'm no thief.

But, they won't stop!

Is it because I'm Black?
Is there a passenger? Is the cab full?

They are empty.

Every time one passes,
he shakes his head 'no' to me.

An hour passes, then an hour and a half.
I wait.

But, not one stopped
because of the color of my face.

NO NATION

No leader, no power, no structural government.

Recruiters of killers,
and weapons of mass destruction.

Children playing in the park,
young imaginations.

Hard to enjoy youth, crucial situation.

Mother gone. Father always been gone. All alone.
Forced to fend for themselves
in the streets they call home.

The streets adopted them,
showed them how to eat.
How to be a man,
and to get it however they can.

That white powder, green leaves,
green paper, dead presidents…
Becomes an enemy, but simultaneously,
more so a best friend.

Ten years old, but thirty in the mind.
Brainwashed. No family.
Parents left them behind.

One death, two deaths, three deaths, four deaths...

But at the rate he's going, he'll only see jail.
A way out of bondage and chains.

No structure. No rules. No nation.

WAR

War with you.

War with me.

War with whites.

War with Blacks.

War with police.

War in my community.

War with guns.

War with identity.

War with economy.

War with everybody.

War on everything.

War with the government.

War with NYCHA.

War with politics.

Government + NYCHA + Politics = Thieves.

War with thieves.

War with beliefs.

War with the mind.

War in these streets.

WAR.

DON'T SHOOT ME

I am a little boy.

I am a little girl.

I am a child.

I am a brother.

I am a sister.

I am a sibling.

I am an uncle.

I am an aunt.

I am a niece and a nephew.

I am a son.

I am a daughter.

I am somebody's child.

I am a husband. I am a wife.

I am somebody's spouse.

I have my hands up. Don't Shoot Me!

THE SHADOWS

Clouded and palled, just a shadow on the floor.

Dark shaded area, just a spot on the wall.

No one notices the silhouettes, outlined shapes.

The contoured lines filled with darkness.

Opaque and obstructed, blockage of light.

Shaded, disregarded, secretly hidden.

Walked on. The forgotten, the most forbidden.

The light increases, the more blurred.

Scary, gloomy… DANGER!

The oppressed, depressed, cast out, excommunicated.

Shut out, turned away, fully obliterated.

Left out, talked about, lack of communication.

Suffering, maliciousness, ostracized with spite.

Destroyed. Covered up.
Always behind in the shadows of light.

"We are nonviolent with people who are nonviolent with us."

- Malcolm X

YOU PEOPLE

Are nasty and look dirty.

Look like criminals,

And all are murderers.

Are rapist, filthy, and you conspire.

All look the same.

Pants sagging, 'ghetto' slang.

Are all on public assistance.

Are drug abusers and dealers.

Live in the 'hood.'

Are all lazy and don't want nothing.

Own nothing, and will continue to be slaves.

Spend all your money on material things.

All you do is have babies at young ages.

Will grow up without anything...

No savings, no inheritance, no school, no education.

Never finish school and end up incarcerated.

Fathers are never around.

How could you possibly do better
in single-parent homes?

Have no ambition and no money to pass down.

Are slowly disappearing,
as soon as the displacement of

Low-income families and small businesses
are wiped out.

DON'T JUDGE ME

Scary looks.

The checking of pockets.

Clutching of purses.

I am not a thief.

Scurried walking.

Question ignoring.

Crosses to the other side of the street.

I repeat, "I am not a thief."

I sit down, you get up.

I hold my hand out,
you place the change on the counter.

I don't have a disease.

I'm simply a human being.

Deep stares, scowls, and dirty looks.

I'm no monster or murderer, and far from a crook.

Door opens, you brush through.

I hold the door, you walk out.

No "thank you." So rude.

I'm not an enemy.

I did nothing to you.

You call me a monkey.

No, I was not raised in a zoo.

I have a name my mother gave to me.

I'm a natural born citizen.

I served my country.

I make an honest living.

I'm a great person to meet.

So, please don't judge me!

THE JURY

The smell of wooden tables.

The sounds from the stenographer.

White judge, all white jury.

Florida state courtroom.

There's no way I'm going home today.

No more birthdays to celebrate.

The whole room is spinning.

I call on God for forgiveness.

Please let them see the evidence.

And not just another "nigger."

I never pulled the trigger.

Short dark hair, about 5'7", shoe size 8.

Size 6, 5'3", long hair straight.

The verdict's in, one hour of deliberation…

GUILTY! GAVEL BANGS.

I don't even fit the description.

WRONGFUL CONVICTION!

YOUNG MAN

Young man, listen and understand.

Keep doing what you're doing,
and you'll end up in the can.

In other words, jail.

You won't be able to afford bail.

Your friends are not your friends,
and will soon become your enemies.

They'll flip to bring you down.

They are going to tell everything.

You're living a life that only loves destruction.

You end up a co-conspirator.

And then, you cop out to the max.

30 years minimum.

Your friend cops to two.

The streets don't love you.

MOMMY

She cooks, cleans, and makes my bed,

Buys my clothes, sometimes I'm fed.

She takes me to school sometimes.

Yells most of the time.

She's here, but distant.

No affection, no emotion, no hugs, no love.

Tells me to get out of her face.

Sometimes I feel misplaced.

She pushes me away.

All I want is her love and attention.

Her hugs and kisses, not to mention.

"What!" Is how she answers when I call.

Sometimes, she doesn't respond at all.

Calls me names and shouts.

Her love is what I doubt.

Why mommy?

WHERE I COME FROM

Where I come from, you live and die young.

Where I from, you pack your side with a gun.

Where I come from, you duck, dodge and run.

Where I come from, the streets are not fun.

Where I come from, there's shootouts and drug spots.

Where I come from, you have to be on watch.

Where I come from, there are no deliveries.

Where I come from, friends turn into enemies.

Where I come from, you're not expected to do good.

Where I come from, they call it the hood.

Where I come from, people die often.

Where I come from, people are soon laid in coffins.

Where I come from, you don't know what it's about.

Where I come from, either you in or you out.

Where I come from, we play the block.

Where I come from, you bound to get knocked.

DISAPPEARING RACE

You rape your women.

You kill your children and siblings.

Murder your friends.

Shoot your brother.

Rob from your mother.

You blame it on the absence of a father.

Drug up your neighborhood.

Spend your life in jail.

Try to bleach your face.

Ashamed of who you are.

You kill off your own people.

Point fingers, never taking the blame.

What a damn shame.

Our people are dying.

Slowly fading away.

Disappearing race.

NIGGER VS. NIGGA

There is no difference in the words.

Pronunciation maybe, but they mean the same thing.

There's no justification, just justifying ignorance.

A double standard of its actual meaning.

Homie, brother, ace, friend.

Dirty, foolish individual, uneducated, disadvantaged.

Trigger and 'trigga' also mean the same thing.

Just different in the way they're pronounced.

"Nigger" and "Nigga" are damaging and hateful slurs.

Adopted by Blacks, but really mean inferior.

Gold chain, slave chain, still shackles around the neck.

Why get so mad?

When certain races say it,
you put them in check.

What makes it ok to say it to one another?

Friendship bond, does that make you my brother?

If it's ok to say, then everyone
should be able to use it.

It was used to tear down a race.

It was said to be mentally abusive.

No matter how one tries to justify
the meaning when it's heard.

"Nigger" and "Nigga" are the same word.

ONCE UPON A TIME

Children used to be children.

Teens used to be teens.

Children used to have dreams.

Teens knew their self-worth,
and took life for its true meaning.

What happened to those days?

Did those dreams fade away?

So wrapped up in social media and games,
while their lives are slowly slipping away.

Man hunt, free home, blind man's bluff.

We had so much fun.

Didn't know times were rough.

Water guns and water balloon fights.

Getting wet at the Johnny pump.

Kickball, baseball, football, basketball.

Skateboarding, sledding, rollerblading.

Follow the leader and remote control cars.

Double Dutch, skelly… Need I say more?

Once upon a time, we used to stay outside,
until the street lights turned on.

We played games too.

But today, games and phones consume you.

Once upon a time…

I wish I could press rewind.

BLACK ON BLACK

First them, now you.

You laugh when I fall.

I thought together we stand tall.

Strong if united, we will be.

Open up your eyes and see.

You curse me with blasphemy.

Wronged me for becoming successful.

Shamed me for being great.

We shared the same pain.

Both whipped by chains.

Martin Luther King Jr. gave us a dream.

Gave us a vision, something never foreseen.

We've been through the same thing.

But, you hate to see me win.

So, deep down,

You are just like them.

WOUNDED CHILDREN

You are a star by far.

Believe in the person that you are.

And who you will become.

People will bully you.

And try to suck you into the negative.

But, just focus on the positive.

Do what's good for you.

In knowledge, there's truth.

Enjoy your youth.

Don't rush to grow up fast.

Or worry about what you don't have.

Just enjoy life.

Stay away from crime.

Sky's the limit, don't give up.

Wounded children listen.

Don't let anyone tell you different.

FATHER

I yearn for your presence.

Mourn your absence.

Is it that you didn't want me anymore?

Was it my fault?

That you left and didn't care for me any more.

I missed you growing up.

You never came to my games.

Where were you when I needed your protection?

Your love and affection.

What? Did I do something wrong?

For you to be gone this long?

I needed your advice, your talks, your warmth.

That man in my life.

I got all A's, graduated, and I'm doing great.

I wish you were there on my big days.

And my sad days.

I needed you to keep me on track.

And steer me away from the bad.

I wish you had shown up for my birthdays.

And coached me for my first date.

I longed for a hug and
for you to say, "It will be alright"
when things were bad, my first fight.

I waited for you to come rescue me.
But, you never came.
I wonder if you loved me the same.

The way that I loved you,
even though you abandoned me.

I longed for a relationship with you.
Wished that I could trade places with my friends.
Because you weren't there, never been.

I hoped to hear your voice,
but never heard a whisper.

Just wanted to hear you, to be near you.
For you to teach me to drive.
I stood there waiting,
hoping you would come by.

Throughout my adulthood, I wanted you near.

Was I that bad that you couldn't be there?

WALK IN MY SHOES

Have you ever tried to walk in my shoes?

Wear my skin tone.

Be mentally abused.

Be defamed and wrongfully accused.

Been turned down or turned away.

Just because you are a darker shade.

Been looked at the wrong way.

Go somewhere where people think you're the same, as the other person, who has a different name.

Kicked out and told you can't perform or entertain.

Or had to sit somewhere because of your race.

Told to go in the back way.

Been forced out or hosed away.

Laughed at because of your body frame.

Or be one of the best and sit out a whole game.

How would you feel to be disengaged?

"We should emphasize not Negro history, but the Negro in history. What we need is not a history of selected races or nations, but the history of the world void of national bias, race hate, and religious prejudice."

- Carter G. Woodson

NO COLOR

No color, no complexion.

All I see are eyes.

The inner soul of an individual is beautiful.

Personality, wisdom, humor.

Everyone bleeds red.

Everyone chases green.

No color.

Unseen.

In the dark, lights out.

Colors faded out.

No one seen.

The imagination of beauty.

Or what you wish one to be.

When we die, body burnt to ashes.

In graves, bodies decay.

Skin fades into bones

All I see are open arms.

Embrace me with your love,
kindness, and inner-self.

Your cheek against my cheek.
Enjoying your warmth and grace.

When I look at you,
I see no color, no race.

LETTER TO THE POLICE

Every day your lives are
at risk to protect and serve.

You've given your life and your time
to protect communities.

You've put your life on the line to protect us
from all foreign and domestic violence.

Every day you have to look
over your shoulder.

Every day you are stuck
with difficult choices that can affect you.

Your work and dedication
does not go unnoticed.

When I'm in trouble,
I look for you to come to the rescue.

When I hear shots,
I listen for your sirens.

When you tell me to stop,
I obey your authority.

I respect the men and women you are.

I admire your courage and integrity.

I value your selfless service.

I adore your dignity and leadership
and I honor what you stand for.

But, I yearn for your respect,
and I hope you don't pull the trigger.

I am an honest citizen.

I've never been in trouble.

I am not a "nigger."

The color of my skin does not define me.

I am not a product of my environment.

I don't sell drugs.

And no, I don't fit the description.

I am your model citizen.

My hands are up.

Don't shoot!

NO MORE FLAGS

What kind of flag do you stand for?

What kind of flag makes you kill your kind?

Hold on, press rewind.

The Black Panthers, The Black Wall Street, The Nation of Islam…

They all stood for something.

Built up our culture and our people.

Didn't kill each other over a flag.

Powerful successors. Educated.

Stood together and marched.

Didn't let outsiders into the community.

Your flag does not bring unity.

It's a divide between our Black culture and nation.

It destroys our people.

Our people who fought for freedom, and a better way of life.

Our ancestors fought so we'd be free today.

But, you influence the bad.

The youth think you're cool,
and even look up to you.

But you own nothing, fighting for the same block.

Fighting for what the government is about to own.

Talking about you own the block.

But, people are purchasing and buying you out.

Matter of fact, they own your city.

Your flag holds no strength.

In jail, it matters the color of your skin.

You have no flag.

And people like you are kin.

All you have is each other.

Inside, they don't care about you
representing your colors.

But you insist on waving your flag.

We are much more powerful as a group,
culture, and nation.

Us sticking together, trust we'll make it!

BLACK LIST

Fitted cap, hoodie on.

Timberlands, jeans, nice jacket.

Nice gold chain, bracelet to match.

Watch and nice gold earring.

Book bag on.

I'm in style.

Fresh and clean, about to start my day.

Cops stop me.

"Hands on the wall!"

They throw me to the floor.

"It's a stop and frisk."

I'm like, *Why they doing me like this?*

"You a drug dealer, huh?"

"Let's see the drugs."

"You look like a thug."

Throw my bag to the floor.

Knock my brand new hat off.

"What you got in the bag?"

They open it up.

It's my work uniform.

Pull my wallet out and see my badge.

I'm one of them...

CONSPIRACY

In 1865, slavery was abolished. Freedom.

No more slave owners. No more picking cotton.
Nor working in a house.

No more transportation in a boat. Sleeping on top of one another. Smelling urine, feces, and dead bodies.

No more rapes, lynching, and fathers
separated from their families.

The whips and chains are gone.
No more Willie lynching and family mixing.

Children forced to be grown men and women.

Integrated schools.

No more side entrances or back of the bus.

Integrated sports.

No more Jim Crow or Brown vs. Board.

Amendments and constitutional rights.
Right to vote, work, and live normal.

No more dog attacks or fire hoses.

Citizenship rights back from birth.

Tuskegee Airmen and Black Wall Street.

Blacks reunited, living free.
Black prosperous communities.

Then hit with a major drug conspiracy.

Like a plague flooded the Black community.
Crack heads, zombies and crack babies.

All for a crack and heroin fix.
Working people turned fiends.

Mothers selling their babies and their bodies.
Drug dealers trying to be the next New Jack City.
The American Gangster.

But in all reality, this conspiracy
was designed to enslave you and me.

The early 1900s was the real crack error. Designed to bring you back, and keep you down forever.

A space for drugs, a slave to fast money.
All designed in this conspiracy.

Glamorizing being at the top. Meanwhile,
killing your own people to get what you got.

All of a sudden, drugs fell in our lap.
Now orange is the new black.

A new way of splitting families.
Black men lost to this drug conspiracy.

This street war lost to jail.

We were doing good before,
with inventions that were stolen…

Historically Black Colleges…
Working classes… Owning land.

Now sons and daughters are visiting
their fathers in a can.

30 years later, and still the same thing.
Making money off Blacks, running a jail ring.

CALL THE POLICE?!

What a shame.
If I were white,
it'd be a different thing.

Call the police?
WHAT? Call the police?!

They don't come when you're in need.
Pull up an hour later,
talking about they were busy.

What do you mean?

It was an emergency!

Drunk guy, vicious dog.
Trapped inside.
Can't even get out into the hall.

Trust in your police department?
Why didn't they come?

Because I live in a housing apartment.

Makes you want to take the law
into your own hands.
But when you do,
you're labeled a violent man.

Trying to protect your family
and where you live.
Trusting in them,

trying to stay positive.

They don't care about us.
To them, you're just another "nigger."

To them, you're a thug,
who doesn't work or hold a job.
They look at you crazy,
but they're the real snobs.

Crooks, drug trafficking,
selling drugs, transporting kids.

Molesting kids, robbing armored trucks,
what the fuck!

Forging tax documents to get more money.

Robbing drug dealers, are you serious?

They're supposed to serve and protect.
Call the police? What the heck?!

They are worse than the scum
they pick up in the street.
But have the nerve to look at me funny.
Such crooked dummies.

They don't want to be bothered
in the Black communities.
This ain't Blue Bloods,
this ain't no TV series.

Call the Police?
Are you "effen" kidding me?!
I'll die before I call 911.
I'd be dead twice before they come!

STRUGGLES

One bedroom, 4th floor.
No living room, no furniture.
Fights and bloody rags in the hall.
Yelling, arguing, hands flying.
One pack of meat in the freezer.
Fiends on every corner.
Crack pipes in the cracks in the ground.
Dirt hills, no playground.
One basketball court.
Guns and shootouts.
Shopping once in a blue.
Everyone looks like me.
One way in and one way out.
Scraping pennies, trying to make 25 cents.
Stealing from stores.
Improvising sports.
Jumping fences.
Hitting rocks with a stick.
Bully or get bullied.
Stay broke or hustle.
Not old enough to work.
Stick up kids.
Fighting for fun.
Struggles.

GROWING UP

Growing up, I wanted to be a gangster.

I wanted people to know who I was
when they saw me, and respect me.
Fear me. Cater to me. Do what I said.

I idolized the gangsters in the movies,
and I dared anyone to cross me.

I wanted the power to have people
do dirt for me at the snap of my finger.

I wanted to stand out in the room
and be the most popular one.

I wanted the control to say what goes,
have the power to move mountains,
and have everyone see it my way.

I wanted the status of a Mob Boss.
To say, "Take care of it" and it was handled.

I wanted all the authority.
Me and only me.

BLACK AND POWERFUL

When you are a top Black icon,
they are scared of you.

You can never stand up for what you believe.
Even for your own people.

Your political views, although correct, are rude.
Now they turn against you and bash you.
Bash you for speaking out, and because
they know you are so powerful.

Why do you think they killed Tupac?
He was becoming too powerful with the truth.
They said, "Nigger how dare you?!"

So they throw dirt on your name.
Try and take your fame.
And try to blackball you.
Oh, how pitiful.

They want the Black men and women we are
To shut up and hold in what we think or believe.
They don't like it, so they want us to retreat.

You stand your ground and hold your own,
Then they do you like they did Nina Simone.
They can't control you, because you are rich.
So they attack, causing you to lose all of it.

Now you have nothing and they leave you dry.
They love to see a "nigger" down or cry.

I have liberties and freedom of speech,
that's what my people fought for.
Now you tell me what I say is uncalled for.

Talk about me like a dog,
because I don't agree with you.
I don't agree with cops killing Black kids.
I'm taking a stand against you.

Standing politically correct is a crime for a "nigger."
They are scared and their fears get bigger.

Before I was famous,
I was and will always be,
Who I Am.

My mother is Black, my father is Black.
I'm a proud African American.

I grew up poor, but now I have money.
Now I say what I say.

You try to take everything from me.
Damn you, cowards!

You think you are the untouchables.
You mad because I'm living like the 'Huxtables.'

I'm Black and I'm proud with my fist in the air.
Whoever don't like it, I don't care!

MEN

Start being a father to your children:

Your girls, so they won't go out hooking for men.
Looking for the love of their fathers that's missing.

Your boys, so they can grow up to be men.
So they won't idolize drug dealers or get influenced.

Teach them how to survive, so that the streets won't
choose how they end their lives.

Teach your daughters how to choose a husband,
and your sons how to choose a wife.

Tell them to put down the guns.
And if they have a problem,
put up their fists and fight.

Teach them how to pick up a book and read,
so they'll leave the guns and drugs in the street.

Teach them how to create their own businesses,
and to watch their 'so called' friends.

Teach them how to shoot a jump shot,
not how to dodge bullets to keep from getting shot.

Teach them how to be parents
and take care of their children.

Let them know they can make it
to the elder age of being grandparents.

Inform them about the value of managing finances,
and the beauty of love and romancing.

Instill in them wisdom and knowledge,
and encourage them to go to college.

To choose a profession and get a degree.
Make them understand that prison
is modern day slavery.

Teach them your roots,
and how to embrace their culture.

Let them know about their Black History.

Let them know you are their number one fan.

Men, step up and become that Man!

WHY?

Why when a Black celebrity
speaks on behalf of their culture, it's a problem?
It's broadcasted all over the news like it's a problem.

But, when white people take over
a federal building, they try and solve it.

Why when the Black Panthers were marching,
they were considered dangerous?

But everybody befriended the KKK,
the white supremacists.

Why when a white person has an M16,
he gets talked to by the police?

But when an unarmed Black kid has his hands up,
he gets shot dead in the streets.

Why when a white man is elected president,
he's brave?

But a Black man, in their minds,
will always be a slave.

Why when a Black man is up,
they attempt to bring him down?

But when a white man kills and slaughters,

the cameras are not around?

Why did the killer of Trayvon Martin
become popular?

Beat trial, nationally known,
killed a Black kid, now a star.

WE SHALL OVERCOME

We shall overcome adversity.

We shall overcome poverty.

We shall overcome violence against
our Black brothers and sisters.

We shall overcome deteriorated
urban neighborhoods.

We shall overcome racism.

We shall overcome division.

We shall overcome white supremacy.

We shall overcome drug-infested communities.

We shall overcome police brutality.

We shall overcome incarceration.

We shall overcome financial deficits.

We shall overcome this economical curse.

We shall overcome capitalism.

We shall overcome social destruction.

We shall overcome the death tolls of young Blacks.

We shall overcome defeat.

WORDS HAVE POWER

The first amendment guarantees
the right to freedom of speech.
But, Black men and women
were crucified for sharing knowledge.

The words of a powerful Black man led to his murder
because his words were too powerful,
and appealed to men and women.
The only way to stop him was to kill him.

Words have power to control a group,
and people building a hierarchy.
But, because the words of a Black man
are so powerful, they used a conspiracy.

Scared that the Black man will rise,
they set up his perfect demise.
An intellectual "nigger" is considered dangerous,
and scares a certain kind.

They infiltrate, trying to influence the minds of
people close to bring down the king from his throne.
Because a Black man promoting peace and love,
they will not condone.

Change the meaning to conspire,
into a terrorist group.
For a group that never used or promoted violence.
But, the power of words was threatened to silence.

FUTURISTIC

Have you ever thought about your future?

Money, wealth, and health…

Investing in stocks and bonds?

Silver, gold, real estate…
Instead of waiting for a Jordan release date.

Have you ever thought about
owning an establishment?

Buying a home, instead of paying rent?

You buy the new style clothing,
and keep up with the latest fashion.

But, did you ever think about owning
your own clothing line, or open up a boutique?
A bodega, a restaurant, or a sneaker store?

Ladies and gentlemen,
you have options to explore.

Stop giving away your money.
When you retire, can you say that
you are going to live comfortably?

Can you say, "I have 10K saved?"

Do you have money for a rainy day?

Do you have equity or assets?

Or, are you living from check to check?

It is better to have Financial Goals,

than to be broke and stuck in prison.
Create futuristic goals to increase optimism.

ADDICTED

On my mind morning, noon, and night.
The smell, that taste.
I feel it on my gums.
On my tongue.
I'm in heaven.
Floating on cloud nine.
Eyes rolling.
Heart pounding.
Licking my lips.
Rubbing myself all over.
Craving for us to be one.
Spending all of my time.
No time for anything else.
No worries.
Got my full attention.
Without you, I'm alone.
You are all I want.
I can taste you.
I'm nodding in and out.
I'm shaking.

I'm cold.

I need you.

Take care of me.

Without you, why live?

I'm addicted.

HARD BEING BLACK

It's hard being Black.

People poke fun and make fun
of Black Lives Matter.

And try to incorporate their worst story.

It's especially hard for Black men.

I always pray that nothing happens to them.
It's like we've been a target since creation.

Hated by all: White, Chinese, Mexican,
Spanish, Black, West Indian.

We are our own worst enemy.

We are part of reciprocity.

Challenged economically.

Looked at differently.

Painted as monsters.

But never do I ever hate the color of my skin.

If I were reborn, I'd choose being Black again.

GUILTY PLEA

Police stop you.
Find an ounce of marijuana in your bag.
You don't smoke.

Straight A student.
College academic scholarships.
Senior year. No kids.

Someone slipped it into your bag.
You get arrested on your way home,
for something that's not yours.

Faced with a felony charge.
A possible sentence of ten years.

Can't afford a lawyer.
Can't afford to do a bid.

Copped out to 730 days.
Community service for one year.

College academic scholarship done.
G.E.D straight out of prison.

When you get out, you can't stay with mommy
in her New York City Housing Development.

Can't vote or serve on any jury
because of "Get Tough" laws by Clinton.

Can't get a job. Don't have enough to live.

No Section 8. No address.

Right back in the system, again.

REST IN PEACE

Bobby Hutton – 1968

Fred Hampton – 1969

Michael Stewart – 1983

Eleanor Bumpurs – 1984

Michael Griffith – 1986

Yusuf Hawkins – 1989

Amadou Diallo – 1999

Malcolm Ferguson – 2000

Patrick Dorismond – 2000

Ronald Beasley – 2000

Earl Murray – 2000

Prince Jones – 2000

Timothy Thomas – 2001

Orlando Barlow – 2003

Ousmane Zongo – 2003

Alberta Spruill – 2003

Timothy Stansbury – 2004

Ronald Madison – 2005

James Brisette – 2005

Henry Glover - 2005

Sean Bell - 2006

De Aunta Terrel Farrow - 2007

Tarika Wilson - 2008

Oscar Grant - 2009

Victor Steen - 2009

Shem Walker - 2009

Kiwane Carrington – 2009

Steven Eugene Washington - 2010

Aiyana Jones - 2010

Aaron Campbell - 2010

Danroy Henry - 2010

Derrick Jones - 2010

Derek Williams - 2011

Reginald Daucet - 2011

Raheim Brown – 2011

Kenneth Harding – 2011

Alonzo Ashley – 2011

Kenneth Chamberlain – 2011

Trayvon Martin - 2012

Ramarley Graham – 2012

Jordan Davis - 2012

SGT Manuel Loggins JR. – 2012

Raymond Allen – 2012

Dante Price – 2012

Johnnie Kamahi Warren - 2012

Nehemiah Dillard – 2012

Timothy Russell - 2012

Melissa Williams – 2012

Wendell Allen – 2012

Shareese Francis – 2012

Rekia Boyd – 2012

Kendrec McDade – 2012

Ervin Jefferson – 2012

Tamon Robinson – 2012

Sharmel Edwards – 2012

Shantel Davis – 2012

Chavis Carter – 2012

Reynaldo Cuevas – 2012

Ramarley Graham – 2012

Deion Fludd - 2013

Kimani Gray - 2013

Kendrick Johnson - 2013

Miriam Carey – 2013

Jonathan Ferrell - 2013

Carlos Alcis - 2013

Larry Eugene Jackson JR. - 2013

Eric Garner - 2014

Victor White III - 2014

Ezell Ford – 2014

Michael Brown - 2014

Tyree Woodson - 2014

Kajieme Powell – 2014

Akai Gurley – 2014

Dante Parker – 2014

Tamir Rice – 2014

Darrien Hunt - 2014

John Crawford III - 2014

Rumain Brisbon – 2014

Jordan Baker – 2014

McKenzie Cochran – 2014

Yvette Smith – 2014

LaQuan McDonald – 2014

****

CHURCH OF FAME – 2015:

Clementa Pinckney

Rev. Sharonda Singleton

Rev. Depayne Middleton-Doctor

Rev. Daniel Simmons SR.

Tywanza Sanders

Myra Thompson

Ethel Lance

Cynthia Hurd

Susie Jackson

****

Freddie Gray – 2015

Sam Dubose – 2015

Sandra Bland – 2015

Cedric Chatman – 2016

Philando Castile – 2016

Alton Sterling – 2016

ABOUT THE AUTHOR

Liz Baker is a Brooklyn born native with a mother who taught her how to survive in this world, and not depend on anyone. Liz is independently strong and able because of her mom. Being raised in a single-parent household brings out a certain kind of fierceness that not everyone can understand.

Liz grew up as a tomboy in the Williamsburg Houses and adopted basketball as her scapegoat. Basketball was Liz's way out, and a chance to get a free education. It opened many doors of opportunity, allowing her to see beyond what she had grown up around. Some people don't make it out and succumb to the pressures of their surroundings. But Liz prevailed, earning a basketball scholarship for Junior High School, High School, and College.

As Liz grew older and saw what was available, she started to think beyond the life of basketball. Liz knew that being a female basketball player couldn't last forever. Therefore, thinking ahead was a must, especially since no one had offered to throw millions on the bargaining table.

Liz Baker is also a proud homeowner, currently striving to accomplish a few more dreams.

Connect with Liz on Facebook at "Poetry of Liz" or email her at PoetryofLiz@gmail.com.

www.ingramcontent.com/pod-product-compliance
Lightning Source LLC
LaVergne TN
LVHW051510070426
835507LV00022B/3023